To

Those who have gone before us

but are forever in our hearts

My Grandma died last night.

Mommy and Daddy said she did.

They said it was her time to go.

Where did she go?

Will she come back?

Can I visit her?

Where's Grandma?

Written and Illustrated by   Judy Vartan

Grandma died last night.

I wonder where she is.

Mommy said,

"She's in the flowers

still blooming in

her garden."

"She's in the stories she read to you so often."

Sally's grandfather died last year.

Sally said he went to Heaven.

I wonder how he got there.

I wonder where Heaven is anyway.

I wonder where you go when you die.

I wonder where Grandma is.

Daddy said,

"She's in the hugs when she came through

the door."

"She's in her smiles while watching you play."

David's uncle died not long ago.

His mother said he'd passed on.

Passed on to where, I wonder.

Did he tell David he was going?

Did he ask David to come visit?

I wonder where my grandma is.

Aunt Mattie said,

"She's in her plum pudding

we bake at Christmas."

"She's in the giggles when

she shared a secret."

Everybody dies sometime,

Mommy and Daddy said.

It is like the flowers that grow, bloom and then are gone.

Everybody dies sometime,

I just wonder where my grandma is.

"She's in the hikes

along the forest trail."

"She's in your tears she wiped away

when Buster died."

Mommy and Daddy said,

"Where's Grandma? Grandma is

everywhere she's been."

"She's in the pumpkins we

carved at Halloween."

"She's in the collection of seashells

from the shore."

"She's in Grandpa's laughter

and the twinkle in his eyes."

"She's in our memories forever

so she's never truly gone."

Grandma died last night.

Last night the moon was full and bright.

I can't see her because she's not

here anymore.

But, all those memories are in my head

and Grandma is in my heart forever.

www.ingramcontent.com/pod-product-compliance
Lightning Source LLC
Chambersburg PA
CBHW041828090426
42811CB00038B/2361/J

*9 7 8 0 9 9 8 6 3 1 7 1 4 *